Merryn McCarthy

PLAYING TRUANT

AGENDA EDITIONS

To dear Kathryn.
How lovely to meet you!
Best wishes with your
writing —
Merryn Mc Carthy

First published in 2010 by Agenda Editions,
The Wheelwrights, Fletching Street,
Mayfield, East Sussex TN20 6TL

ISBN 978-0-902400-91-7

Front cover painting: *Nameless Road* by **Michael Flaherty**.
Michael Flaherty comes from County Kerry, Ireland. His work
can be found in Greenlane Gallery, Dingle, Co. Kerry, Ireland.
www.greenlanegallery.com

Merryn McCarthy lives in Sussex, having grown up in Ireland and Southern England. She has run English Departments for most of her teaching career.

She was winner and runner-up in the Robin Lee poetry prize at Sussex University (1992/3), where her thesis on walking and writing received acclaim and is housed in the university library.

Her poems have appeared in *English* (O.U.P.), *The Irish Press*, *Agenda*, and *Sussex University Press*. This is her first full-length collection.

For Kim and Kerry

Acknowledgements

Some of these poems have appeared in *English* (Oxford University Press), *Agenda* and *Sussex University Press*.

Hamlet: *But what, in faith, make you from Wittenburg?*

Horatio: *A truant disposition, good my lord.*

Contents

Shut the Classroom Door

Out of Bounds

Word from the Other Country

Shut the Classroom Door

Convent School

From this womb,
this stone sepulchre
I will emerge.

Light filtering through
casts shadows
on my skin.

Outside a car coughs,
a white dove flutters –
otherness, space.

I am canopied, controlled,
still at the centre
but pulsating.

A gradual impulse
as arches, doorways
betray movement;

candles flicker,
music trembles
to burst forth.

This place speaks
of beginnings and endings,
happiness and heartbreak.

It is eternal,
too certain now –
I need to break out.

Shut the Classroom Door

Shut the classroom door quietly.
I'm outside now but still there
in the head of the girl
fascinated by language and story,
the boy passionate about poetry,
all those who experienced
the transforming power of imagery –
and even in the one
who simply looked up
through the high windows
at trees shedding leaves,
turning into broomsticks
to sweep me gently away
for both of us to pursue
our uncertain but necessary journey.

Fingersmith

Water trickles over lustrous light.
I enter caves of thought,
landscapes of feeling
where moulded clay evolves
beyond cell, cloister,
potter's wheel, to purpose, meaning.

You give me words, texture,
colour of all shades
that erupts in burnished golds
or blues melting into greens.
Smoked pots uncoil
in swirls and windings,
glazes of tin, lead, antimony.

Art finds its roots here
in the clay that formed us,
the dust of our dying.
I am grounded by stoneware,
terracotta vessels, plates,
or propelled heavenwards
over mud-hued bas reliefs
of seas and estuaries.

Fingersmith, it is I
who am urged to ingenuity,
creativity, fired
by your touch.

Head of Classics at Pompeii

for Maria

Cassandra,
you speak
in the gods' tongue,

your voice
lapidary
as light.

Shards, stones
of knowledge
at the cutting edge.

Cassandra,
the city
your mosaic.

You plot
our path
in the cross-currents

of time
to dine
with the dead.

In your world
of absolutes,
our uncertainty.

Your words
swell
in warning.

Cassandra,
guide
to the underworld,

here
on the towpath
you stride ahead.

Chemistry Lesson

The high priestess
leads the ritual
like an immolation.
Her vestal virgins,
perfectly self-possessed,
deflect observation
as they calculate
their chances, weigh up,
all known essences
at their command.

There is purity
in their movements,
their sequences:
they take temperatures,
fill up glass vials,
empty them slowly,
then wash their vessels
out in water,
replace them on shelves,
wipe their hands.

Each aqueous solution,
each result
escapes detection
like poisoning.
It is all so
deftly choreographed
and executed,
so carefully planned.

Playing Truant

Sunny day –
you exist
outside plans,
timetables, interviews,
huge certitudes.

The blood
is calmer now
that rises
at injustice,
all fingers
on the pulse.

And the voices
that want
to be heard,
drumming, drumming,
yearning to mastermind
a revolution.

Why do they
get it so wrong,
the geniuses
with their ready
calculations?

I have played
this game
too long,
never quite
fitting in,
dangerous

with my dreams
and desperations.
The bells
are ringing
as I escape.

Hauntings

Hardy's Eustacia Vye

It is the rustle of her dress
over the heath that haunts me,
her drawn-bonnet of silk
so out of place
as she seeks the sun,
the desperations that light
so many fires.

It is the moon's eclipse
at her wooing like the hood
that shadows her beauty,
or that hoary night
when, in the attire
of a Turkish knight, she trod
frost blades to duel with love.

It is she on whom all doors
close, love blighting;
fateful misunderstandings,
spun in circles at the gipsying,
only her seducer to turn to.
The moon again risen –
her strange, trance-like state.

Vulnerable in a nightgown
at her morning mirror,
it is the heavy coil of hair
she drops as he enters
to accuse her, caught
like the moth in the candle,
all colour drained from her face.

It is his love's desperate wait,
every sound her footfall,
the break of her soul's wings.
It is her red neck-ribbon
and unlaced sandals
witching her to whirlpools,
cloaking her in night.

Folly

King Lear in the garden,
the full glare
of the afternoon.

Hannah brings cherry strudel
and two-chocolate mousse
gashed with strawberries.

We go through
the middle scenes of madness
juggling pens with plates,

verse with prose.
King Lear and cakes.
They strip off in the heat.

Now they will forever
recall the comic grotesque,
understand the folly.

Visiting Chenonceau

He promised me
a fairytale château
straddling a river.

At the Gare du Nord
head and shoulders
above the crowd,

my son. We bumped
over the cobblestones,
left-hand drive

out of the city,
skirting Proust's Combray
to pause at Chartres.

Spangles of light
from the rose window
stained the floor.

Madonna and child.
He smiled as I lit
a candle to his future.

The sun blazed
our way south,
crossing Loire, Cher

to a lesser river.
Islands, sandbanks
beached us. Lovers,

riders ambled past.
The current flowed
over shining pebbles,

birds culled the silence.
Through distant trees
turrets soared.

Leavetaking

I was teaching Yeats,
his obsession with beauty,
transience, old age –
All that's beautiful drifts away
Like the waters.

She called me to sister her
at the door of death.
I arrived as a stretcher
was borne down the steps
of the Georgian colonnade.

It was almost staged:
the ambulance waiting,
a husband standing,
her daughter a guide
as she crossed over.

Sedated, she did not know
that I followed
all the way –
the river coursing by,
my music playing.

She passed like a queen,
too young, still beautiful,
while I survive
to fight the current
in her wake.

Escapade

At Toussaint, half-term, our reckless night drive
through rain and whipped-up leaves,
the whole of France spinning in our wake.
The sun tremulously piercing morning mists,
daylight halo bright in turning trees,
our passion all absorbing.

The great Dordogne in flood below us,
all was ours – smoke wafted from your Gauloise;
you brought me warm bread, local wine, cheese.
From the river, driftwood which defined us.

I scent you still across the lost years,
always the physical tremor, the heartache,
travelling a known French road in search of you.

Gap Year

Inside, pages turn.
Outside, gold spill
of autumn leaves.

I wake to a new rhythm:
a car speeding by,
bird fall from eaves.

Days spread out
like water swelling
on a full tide.

Sunlight, fernlight
before shadows thicken,
then firelight, flame,

and a curious
spying of the land
in between,

allowing things
to happen involuntarily.
Learning to be guilt free.

That World

That world
was a walk away,
a hill climb
there and back
three times a day.
Bright young faces
opening like flowers,
high windows
the sun poured through.
First snow, violent showers:
we wrote all weathers.

I was the centre.
All looked to me
to give, draw out,
determined to be
creative, different.
That world
was a quest.
I travelled with so many
just beginning their journey
as mine, very gradually,
drew to an end.

Striding Out

'I am a stride at a time.' James Joyce: *Ulysses.*

The world at its most beautiful,
perhaps, carved in frost.
All is whitened
in my striving.

A brittle sun and blue sky
sharpen my focus.
Each leaf, branch, tree,
defined, magnified.

Surface patterning shot
as in close-up,
like the fine cracks
of a face marked and lined.

Behind me, my workplace
on the hill, the gatehouse
with its entrances and exits,
high sash windows

facing west which watch me
coldly, dispassionately,
striding into the brilliance
of a January day.

Is it the winter
that conspires with me
as I walk away?
Edward Thomas sets the pace,

Virginia Woolf, both Wordsworths,
all the great walkers;
we brave lonely lanes,
woods, long fields.

I am spurred on
to acceptance, to translate
into words gleaned wisdoms,
following the writer's way.

Luminosity

Suddenly the sun comes out.
A dog barks as a couple walk by
and a tractor chugs up the hill.

From its perch on the table
a wagtail lifts and dips into the pool,
and we emerge from the gloom.

They say poets travel the dark roads,
but the ways here are chalk white,
draw out inner light.

The Map is a Flower

The map flowers
in front of me,
the city its corolla.

Sun spills over
the North Downs,
Samuel Palmer country.

I note its hill,
still bright,
but no sheep

or magic apple tree,
before the tunnel
obscures all light.

Man is free, said Voltaire,
at the moment
he wishes to be.

I propel myself forwards,
needing to reach
named places anonymously.

Out of Bounds

Trespasser

My first spin
on a new bike.
School half term:
no-one around
on all that
deliciously smooth tarmac.

I am a ghost rider
in a ghost town.
I take in details
I never did when
walking up and down
between lessons.

My reflectors glowing,
I delight in
my abandonment
on the forsaken site.
Learner, not teacher,
I go through

all the gears,
then free wheel
as I circle bat-like,
trespasser or thief,
stalking my own shadow
over hallowed ground.

Eye Test

Besuited, double-barrelled,
he shakes my hand.
Black clouds float
across my vision,
the blurs and shadows
of unequal eye contact.

Explorer now, with probes
and searching lights,
he crawls over
my eye's wall.
Domes and bulbs
burst in my head.

He is the first
to touch, reach
my retina. He describes
my nerve hole,
then raises
his flag of conquest.

Gouaches

viewing Turner at Petworth

i

Turner was right –
there are many ways
of capturing the moment,
refracted through light:
the subtle radiance
of a glance, shine of eye.
A hand fine-boned, burnished,
poised for touch. The surprise
of rose-tint within neutrals,
or sudden black against grey.
No matter the rain:
always the ray
directed through glass
in Chinese white.

ii

The colours are luminous,
blended to opacity,
but always a red tint
or hue – the mingling
of pleasure and pain.
In these high, dark rooms
furnished with oils,
clouds and line of downs
distant through Georgian frames,
we warm to the complicity
of colour, those spots of light.

iii

All the things
that cannot be said
are here translated
this watercolour day,
the hand wielding the brush
finding the light.
We move with formality
from room to room
into the landscaped garden.
The importance of ritual
to be able to arrive.
And the path chalked out,
a ring of trees on the summit,
his encircling arm.

To a Great Grandmother Kingsley

I follow in the wake
of your rebellion,
your discarded silk slippers
and heavy crinoline.

I boot myself firmly
as you did for escape
from laced-up convention,
find my feet

in your stackyard
gathering sheaves, not heirlooms,
trampling on straw,
inhaling the sweet hay.

Family outcast for eloping
with your farmer,
you gave birth, kept faith
with the proud books

that someone passed on,
and etched on a caul
a hieroglyph of heredity
whose identity I would learn.

Imagined Grandmother,
impulse of my exploration,
my unleashed tongue.
I need to write you back

into history, to gift me
with my bloodright.
Through life-lines
and fertile fictions,

your maiden name
with your brothers'
in lasting print,
bright, leather-bound.

Rodmell River

The river curves
its calligraphy
across the valley,

footnotes of
borstal track,
barrow down.

Torque-like
it clasps me
to its flow.

Swollen water-line,
stranded
to a siren pitch,

tongued and forked
reaches
of estuary.

Ebb and flow
of moon,
she is wearing out

the waters.
Iridescent scars
of an unmasked face.

Whirlpool
of stars,
my night's cauldron.

River
winding me
in its tortuous embrace.

Out of Bounds

Virginia Woolf on the Sussex Downs

Over the Downs' bare back
ripples of light and shade,
the undulating rhythm
of your walking pace.

Transgressing plot and path
you stride beyond
all bounds where blackthorn
blooms white spray
where, lift and fall,
the land's chalk swell
releases vision.

You stalk them here,
those separate selves,
to find on foot
the impulse of your quest,
unity of being.

Each step's a forward pace
for pen on page,
to the last dip
where pattern breaks
in a rush
and crash of waves.

Footsteps

Mary Wollstonecraft in Scandinavia 1795

Surefooted, you tread
uneven roads,
paths private, overgrown,
which snag and pull
your hitched-up
eighteenth century skirts.

Barefoot on rocks
you siphon strength
from sun, sculpting
certainties, space,
even at the cliff's edge
of strange lands.

You write with bird's quill,
pulsing wrist, flights
which reach to the quick,
from any couped-up
chamber recess,
wayside inn.

Your outraged voice
breaks ice beyond
a frozen river
where women stoop
to wash the linen
with cracked and bleeding hands.

Solitary walker,
your summer is imprinted
on all futures.
Like new-born hopes,
your daughter's tiny
footsteps on the sands.

Dorothy Wordsworth

Grasmere, 1802

Each morning, note,
before she walks out
for the word,
she bakes, washes
and starches,
hangs out the linen.

Each evening, watch,
she dares the curve
and muscle of each path
and meets above the lake
the moon, her mirror.

Each glittering leaf
and twig observed, defined,
back she walks;
transcribes her luminary
poet's vision
in daily, footsprung rhythm.

Playing Hookey

Mayfield College 1868 – 1998

They learned to grow cross-country
at the kissing gate,
beyond Heronry Wood
and the cherry tree ride,
fording Furnace Brook
before the uphill climb to Mayfield.
The school had lost its landmark tower,
but through all their rebel years
they knew the way.

Ghosting the footpaths now
where ways and waters meet,
they stalk each other
or, lost to prefects, light up
in huddled groups among the trees.
Their voices echo
from the woods
forever exploring, forever young,
wading up stream, playing hookey.

Scavenger

Frost-bedevilled day.
All is hard,
worn to bone.
A once muddy path
encrusted.
At the wood's edge
mewing seagulls
forage on waves
of whitened furrows.

Leaves glint as I search
for twisted shapes
to keep or burn:
wood hoard.

The ride protected
with hornbeam, holly,
but further back
ancient rotted trunks.
A blackened spear
breaks off, exposing
the tree's core,
a pleated column
dried to a husk.

As I pull it becomes
an angel's wing,
rose patinated,
unfeathered, smooth
between its ribbing.
There is a light crackle,
a stirring as if
from arboreal bonds,
decades of sleep.

I bear my prize
proudly, carefully,
and leave it
at the hearthside
in rippling folds,
emblem of wanderings,
guardian of home.

Nuns arrive in Mayfield, Sussex 1872

When you arrived
there were hops
on the hillside,
as yet no train
puffing across the valley,
only horses plodding
up unmade roads.

Nobody noticed
at first the flutter
of black veils,
the clink of beads,
the busy feet.

But suddenly
from the ruins
of the Archbishop's palace
a sound of singing,
so other-worldly
and sweet, broke
the silence of centuries.

Strand House, Rye

No more the sea.
Only the hidden river
which scribbles its way
across the marshes,
past a white windmill
to harbour here
on the old quay.

Below the perched town
a busy ring road, yet
masts attest to moorings
and, behind fishing huts,
cafés, tourist shops,
Strand House, its name
proud still in gold.

It is bow-shaped,
weatherboarded, as if
for long-term beaching,
inside stripped back
to the bone, furniture
skeletal as driftwood
or worked in unbleached hemp,
handwoven linen.

Industrial spotlights
straddle the floor
like sailors settled in
for nights of drinking.
Juke boxes plucked
from post-war joints
play flashbacks
over purple-velvet seating.

No more the sea,
though gulls wheel overhead
and all feels holiday,
different. At the tail end
of Mermaid Street,
you almost expect
to hear singing.

The Art of Rococo

For Eileen

Sink deep into your bergère,
play at being a Marie-Antoinette,
a shepherdess!

You greet me self-mockingly
by day in your salon,
never a sick room,

a scarf covering your head.
*'It's great what a little make-up
can do,'* you say.

This long night I see
how the moon gilds,
casts light on darkness,

every leaf, flower or tree
softly muted, faded
like old silk or tapestry.

Facing me now,
your bloom lost too soon,
your audacity lifts my despair.

Il Faut Toucher
Aimé Maeght

It was always *do not:*
do not touch, keep off.
But when you grasped
a branch as you climbed
you felt how the tree
conspired to support you,
sensing its living sap,
the sun's heat
behind rough bark.

Now I learn from the sun
as it works its alchemy
of gold on autumn leaves,
or weaves through poplars
a translucent gauze.
And from my artist friend
who shows that even
fingers dipped in paint
can magic vision.

To see *il faut toucher*
handwritten on display
at an exhibition,
is to capture such irony
where textured paper, mobiles
of Miró, Calder, Giacometti,
Braque, teach creativity
through childish joy,
playful transgression.

Assignation

Spring: the ancient pear tree
bursts into blossom.

Beside the Seine
I find an odd volume
in pitted leather –
1796. Paris,
Les Liaisons Dangereuses.

I see him emerge
from the church
of St. Sulpice,
bag in hand.
A sudden bound
down the steps
as she appears,
breathless, from nowhere.

Their total embrace,
momentary, illicit,
reverberates
like gun shot,
bird flight.

Word from the Other Country

Words First

It is words I remember
first – stories and spells
transfixing moments,
ports of call for memory
that still bring a father

home from sea.
Never far inland, he took us
over stiles and streams,
playing at obstacles,
rehearsing changes,

even his death, with surprises.
He chanted magic in fields
which rounded in oranges.
Words as sudden findings
derived from wizardry.

Through his dragon tales
our mother traced
her own patterns,
rhythms and rhymes
to earth enchantments.

Penelope to all
his wanderings,
her own yearnings woven
into his seafarer's quest,
their joint adventure.

Through games of chance
his nine lives, till fate
struck on land. Tide-borne,
she carried him back:
she the moon on water,

tale bearer. His sagas
stored away she resurrected
mythologised, aromatic as linen
from her camphorwood chest.
Horizons shimmer beyond death.

Word from the other Country

In the review
I am reading,
Word from the other Country,
a poet has your name.

Heartache returns
in a rush.
Everything separates us
but first love

shared, its surge.
And later, the gift
of a son.
Then singleton.

You were the rebel
I admired
with a heart.
Labour party, donkey jacket,

roll your own,
film noir,
the Rolling Stones.
All I hadn't been.

Your particular scent
and boyish charm
all I had longed for
and never known.

Labelled for years
with your name,
my sad eyes
still betray

a loss of identity.
Never again at home
in any country.
Never again wholly sane.

Knocking at the Door

There is always a jolt,
a reminder to catch
at the present.
Light reflecting
from the high windows
of my mother's house,
knowing she is
no longer there.

My son's childhood painting
of the whole
lopsided building,
newly framed for a sister
at Christmas to keep
it just so: door,
shutters waiting
to be opened
on her smiling face.

May Day

On a train
as in childhood
wrapped in
your fur-coated love.
White may blossom
on the hedges,
bluebells going over.

A circuitous route
with a line closed,
like our trip
for your pacemaker check
when you laughed
at the side track,
the adventure.

Then later, in a cutting,
when I looked out
through trees
screening the hospital
where you lay
in one of your attempts
at dying, my heart

clenched as always
at the distance
when I owed it to you
to be holding your hand.
And your last gasp
which I missed
by minutes,

running too late.
But my father's voice
halloos still
from the far end
of the station.
He smiles gleefully now
after such a long wait.

Mermaid Rose

To my mother

Mermaid, you unfold
your heart
at my window,

vibrant as song.
You have wound
your way

to this stillness,
accepting sandbanks
and shores.

Fragile in the sun,
your hair whiter,
your head haloed

in Autumn light,
you watch
for the tide.

Spellbound, you see
mist lifting
from the hills,

valleys brightening,
unleashed waves
of land.

Your beauty
a mirror
where two worlds meet,

your fragrance
wafting
beyond time.

Crescent Moon

Tonight the crescent moon
is cradled in night.
You lie in the hospital
drifting. I hold you,
stroke your forehead,
note your unlined skin,
curve of cheek,
arch of nose.
Your fine long limbs,
the thumb I have inherited.

Seeing you beautiful
to the end, I weep.
Nearly a century now
your shining, bestowing
light through dark,
illness, strife. Tonight
the world moves on,
but the moon, drawn,
to a sliver, lies
cradled in sleep.

Adagio

From Beethöven's Hammerklavier Sonata

Sitting tall in his sixteen years,
he raises the lid on exposure.
In this performance
he is himself far more
than in any small talk.
He mouths unconsciously
the plaintive adagio,
tonguing his cheek
as his grandfather did
with each copperplate stroke.

He plays from memory
time's uneven agony,
the rising cadence
evocative, sad.

'The old form must admit
a new', Beethöven said,
as major becomes minor
with adolescent ease.
His fingers hammer home
present urgency, the complexity
of theme: dull marching
of bass notes, the treble
still singing. His hands find
all reaches of the dream.

Player and music fuse,
float, harmonies vibrate.
And bolder chords forged
in the sonata's measured wake.

Witch's Hat

For Patsy

Madcap in a witch's hat
you bedevil straight paths
and simple ways.

In your canter you tie
witch-knots for survival,
chant family lays.

Once I sank knee-deep
in mud. In sleep
you muttered prayers

to allay my dares.
Your plangency
plucked at my temerity,

the forest encircling
our nakedness.
But as we danced

to its reaches,
the sun glared.
Breach born

we crossed worlds
to become strangers,
at home in each,

our presents colliding
in lost loves
and skeined scars.

In an airport
you collapsed, premonitor
of our father's last breath.

For him, well-booted,
it was a final passage,
but you remained

in transit for ever,
learning to treat
vehicles with disrespect,

needing only a piano
to play largos
to his unattended death.

Now from the ducking-pond
of despair you gasp
for life, relive dramas,

your sybil's voice
casting his magic
in relentless tunes

to make wizards of weaklings
and graft old perfections
onto new moons.

Epiphany

You left the house
carolling *Three Kings,*
the tree still fresh
from rain,
holly and ivy,
a surfeit of berries
and garlands
of heart-shaped leaves.

A walk to the waterfall
in the woods –
And this the quest
of the travellers three...
Water sounds murmuring
at the edge of day.

Wearing your coat
I bring in logs
you have stacked
for my winter.
Star of mercy,
star of grace –
the comfortless
body of night.

An inchoate dawn,
the outside light imploding.
The Kings are travelling
Freezing ice on the motorway's
long blade.

In the airport's
neon glare,
just one monstrous tail
looming on the runway.
Travel with them!

The sun is a clear orb
suspended in mist,
a desert sun.
Offer thy heart –
Your voice resounds.
As I drive home,
a flock of birds
takes flight.

Air Mail

Your letters fall
like wind-blown flakes
out of sequence
and time.
How can I collate
your distance
in a winter
which exposes
the bone of anguish
in absence so raw.

Each stump
and bough of tree
shoulders its burden.
Knee-deep in snow
my helpless hands
shift white layers
which envelop
your existence.
Flurries of panic
ice up with no thaw.

All night sleep
drifts. I listen
as if to a baby's breath
for the boiler's steady beat.
Peering from eaves
sharp-fringed
where morning hangs
in crystal phials,
I wait for your words
to settle at my feet.

Blackbird

Blackbird, yellow beak,
green tree, snow.

One piece of bread
on white below.

Drifts in arms of branches,
nuptials of snow.

He's on the magnolia
said not to flower.

But I remember a blossom
whose scent could overpower.

Bird on the tree
I brutally lopped,

now a bower
though all singing has stopped.

Blackbird and I
this side of the wall.

Out there more snow
on the world will fall.

I go about my business,
turn my back on the tree

where a round, round eye
still looks at me.

His beak is dark yellow,
the snow is deep.

Behind my thick-paned window
I start to weep.

His sharpness pierces me
like his beak the bread.

But suddenly with the snow
he's gone, he's fled!

And then

And then I looked up
and saw you,
dryad, faun,
southern, sun-bronzed
escaped from the woods
of my dreams.
The same half-smile
on your lips,
that cloud of hair,
the enigmatic glance
that leaves me
too human,
shelved in air.

Gauloise

Sanely sifting routine
papers into file, all
tokens lost in my
equivocating hands,
I taste a bitter almond
tang and tongue my
mouth's resonance for
sharp recall. It is a
fresh essence of leaf
whose pungency restores,
encapsulating bliss.
I inhale a feeling,
scent a presence.
Long summers unfurl
in smoke clouds strong
with the pang of love.
I grasp the packet
firmly, its edge of silver
deftly peeled; each white
roll holds its promise
intact, like Spring, which
leaves fragrance, not ashes,
redolent of you.

Shorthand

i

Your writing unearths you
like chalk on ploughed land.
What you say is high voltage,
lightning in my hand.

ii

The sea unscrolls itself,
runs, runs to shore.
Deep under the water
where the waves
pulled me down,
your hold still sure.

iii

You walk towards me
then away
in small leaps and bounds.
No more letters.
Only cryptic notes,
guarded signs,
and crying sounds
between the lines.

iv

Only you know
my beads of memory,
know why I have strung
a necklace of names
around my throat.
Only you know
that it strangles me.
See how it glitters
in supplication!

v

I wrote reams for you,
walked miles to rendez-vous,
endured your distance.
You plucked beauty
from me like a prize.
Your letters, catching
at the heart
of injury, consoled, kindled,
unleashed our fire.
This was the art
of correspondence.
Those passionate,
immortalised days
that we now betray.

vi

For my name
there is fresh ink
in your pen.
Even as you waver,
two letters join.
Then without pausing
you indulge in
a long cursive tail
before the final n.

Rapunzel

From over the hill
you come
bringing daylight,
calling my name.

I let down my hair.

How agilely
you climb up
to meet me,
fiercely reaching,
strongly holding.

We step wide-eyed
into noon's
open spaces,
switchbacks
of day.

I follow you
at dusk.
Your long wave
back over
the hill.

Night separates.

But dawn
finds me waiting
for your bright
coming.

I would bind you,
wind you
in hair.

Circe

Circe, your eyes dark
with island secrets
draw suitors in.
Glaucous as ripe grapes
they bloom features

sharpened by sun, mistral,
nasals of Mondragon,
Madrague: sea-names
resonant as sails tacking
westwards from Ionian isles,

Massalian holds crammed
with family ties and
tales bound to your
purpose, the stamp
of convention on contraband.

Your brew is pungent
with lotus leaves, lavender
neat from Southern
slopes, virgin olives,
black-whiskered wheat.

Deep-cauldroned spells
linger in your memory,
seductions of sailors
married to spring tides,
stranded wives spinning

away knowledge, fears.
More nearly secure,
loom whirring, you mime
motions of marital bliss,
mouth your rhymes

to those eager for adventure,
winter-warmth, who succumb
to the Siren song rising
in their credulous ears,
deaf to the passage of years.

You wind them in –
confident in your craft:
outworn marriages like
ships, not wrecked
but snugly in draught.

They play cat's cradle
with your lures
among calanques and rocks
as you tease out yarns
from your replenished stocks.

Seahorse

I came from the sea
on tidal ebb and flow
to earth my meaning,
foaling my beliefs
in flower-filled fields,
inland reaches.

Trespasser, I swished
through tunnels in long grass,
sorrel flames flanking me,
my shadow moving beside me.

I caused barking of fox cubs,
tortoiseshell swarms of butterflies –
warmed to sun-baked harmony,
wrapped in hill and down.

But wind over wheatfields
rippled like waves,
tugged at my mane,
played with my tail.

Moon and clouds scudded
in space above me.
Dewfall dampened,
hedges confined.

I yearned for past flow
and fluency, the ocean's urgency
to unleash me
from this beaching,
salt sharp in my nostrils,
on my uncurbed tongue.

Half Irish

I watch you quietly
serve out the spuds
to English schoolboys
as if to strangers,
dark eyes lowered
reserving your pride.

Confident they come
from the chapel
where Pugin angels
play harps, where
missionary saints
close the divide.

Holding no faith,
you armour yourself
against their brightness,
bridling your inheritance
which labels you foreign,
a name to hide.

From birth an outsider
unfairly untouched
by education, kitchen boy
inside their pantry,
all they have hoarded
for the chosen tribe.

A nomad, you know
the rise of hills,
rough seas, a mirage
of homelands, but find
through such ferrying
a footing on each side.

Smile as you dish out
the spuds; show them
how easily you cross
camps and borders.
Sculpt your identity
in what you unite.

Emigrant

His foreign accent
confused, drew hatreds
that cut and bled like
deracination, crossings
of blood and decease.

Marooned, he took bearings.
sounded depths, salvaged
testaments to unravel
a skein of Irishmen, Wild Geese.

In odd corners they turned up:
missals, fiddle-cases, proud
inscriptions on fly leaves
forged in copperplate, gold.

Taking French leave from drill
and desk, he winked
at rival empires, trade winds,
dealing in currencies of seas.

His wings clipped by bigots,
he signed away life insurances,
learning that kings can be
dispossessed, stone castles

turn to air. Cocking his hat,
he navigated through
sailors' tongues, English,
Arabic, Portuguese.

He played pennywhistles
for a breeze, the ocean
of Celtic spirals
he bequeathes.

Burial at Sea

A strange world
of indeterminate colour,

brightness in a void
glazed by the sea:

sunspot shifting the shadow
on the wave-heave,

swung into rhythm.
Salt-bleached, the horizons

fade in the wash.
The cool domes of our eyes

are blurred by tears
that taste of salt,

our moods fickle as the sea.
Turning, turning is the wheel

of the ship – and the mind
with the world. Bird

after bird rides the wind,
calling. Whitely

each wing-tip curving
defines purely the arc

in whose movement
we are still.

The Piping

Riding the Solent to Lee,
the waves broke
at the sailors' piping.
It was too deep
to see him gone –
riding the Solent to Lee.

O Seasons, O Châteaux

After Rimbaud

O seasons, O châteaux.
Through trees, sudden spires.

For summers long past,
autumn's slow fires.

Landscape an emotion,
magic a certainty –

and such beauty.
Now a broken spell.

O seasons, O châteaux!

Shrouded in mist,
a spectre of intensity,

dying in the moment
of its dark farewell.

Burial Grounds

i

Daylight is hooded
in downland
talon-edged,
chalk on stone.
Death's tenure
is certain here
where barrows bruise,
baring bone.
Strange solace
of sea-lapping,
ash-scattering
wind moan.

ii

The naked hills
expose me to
my winding sheet
of rain; sheer fall
of sun, moon, sky.
Stripped of shelter
I knock at the door
of long-buried lords.

iii

At dusk
the river snakes
to the sea.
It is late
our descent
and speaks
of endings.
Wordlessly
we search
our pockets.
A coin
for the ferryman,
to cross.